Volume 3
The Church of Jesus Christ

**A year's worth of simple messages
that can be given during Primary
or Family Home Evening**

Tiny Talks

Volume 3
The Church of Jesus Christ

A year's worth of simple messages
that can be given during Primary
or Family Home Evening

By Tammy & Chad Daybell

Illustrated by Rhett E. Murray

CFI

Springville, Utah

ISBN: 1-55517-672-0
e. 2

Published by CFI
Imprint of Cedar Fort Inc.
www.cedarfort.com

Distributed by:

Cover design © 2003 by Lyle Mortimer
Illustrations © 2002 by Rhett E. Murray

Printed in the United States of America
10 9 8 7 6 5 4 3 2 1

Printed on acid-free paper

Table of Contents

Introduction

As parents, we have experienced the challenge of writing Primary talks that are simple enough for our children to read, but that are interesting to the children in the audience. To help other parents in our situation, we have created the *Tiny Talks* series.

Volume 1 is linked to the 2002 Primary theme of *Temples*, while the theme of Volume 2 is *The Savior*. It was written to help Primary children understand the mission of Jesus Christ and grow closer to him.

This third volume is tied to the 2003 Primary theme *"I belong to the Church of Jesus Christ of Latter-day Saints."* Many stories in this volume come from the childhood experiences of the modern prophets. We have purposely focused on stories involving the more recent prophets, particularly Spencer W. Kimball, Ezra Taft Benson and Howard W. Hunter.

These stories are entertaining and often include a hint of humor, but more importantly, they show what it means to be a young member of the Church of Jesus Christ of Latter-day Saints. Hopefully the children of the Church will gain a greater appreciation for these great men who have served as our prophets.

These talks can be used in many settings, including Family Home Evening. If a talk is used in Primary, we suggest the child give the talk while holding up the picture at the appropriate time. The child could conclude with a short testimony about the topic, and close by saying, "In the name of Jesus Christ, amen."

At the end of some of the talks you will find small footnote numbers. These correspond to the list of sources at the back of the book.

We have found that visual aids greatly enhance a talk. With each talk we have listed pictures that could be used from the Gospel Art Picture Kit (GAPK). It is available from the Church Distribution Center. If you don't have one, your meetinghouse library might have a set. The meetinghouse library may also have other pictures available that fit the talk.

Thank you for your support of this project.

Tammy and Chad Daybell

Chapter 1

I belong to The Church of Jesus Christ

Jesus organized the Church

Scripture:

And they who were baptized in the name of Jesus were called the church of Christ.
(3 Nephi 26:21)

Visual Aid:
GAPK #211
Jesus ordaining the apostles

Everyone who lives on the earth is a child of our Heavenly Father. We lived with him before we came to earth. He loves us, and has sent us to earth so we can someday become like him. One of our spirit brothers, Jesus Christ, was chosen to become our Savior, and as we follow the teachings of Jesus, we can return to live with Heavenly Father.

Sometimes life on earth isn't easy, and we need to be taught right from wrong. For that purpose, Heavenly Father has always had prophets on the earth to teach people the gospel plan, such as Adam, Enoch, Moses, and Nephi. But when Jesus was born in Bethlehem, the true teachings had been lost for many centuries.

The Savior organized the true church. It was called the Church of Jesus Christ. The Savior ordained twelve apostles and they preached the gospel to others. Many people knew the apostles were teaching the truth, and they wanted to join the church. The apostles baptized these people. Little children were especially welcome in the church, and Jesus would give them blessings. Heavenly Father was happy the true gospel was on the earth again.

2

Peter was chosen to be the prophet

Heavenly Father had given Jesus many special priesthood powers. When Jesus organized his Church, he gave this priesthood to the twelve apostles, who were the leaders of the church. The apostles needed the priesthood so they could perform special ordinances such as baptism, giving the gift of the Holy Ghost, and blessing the sacrament. This priesthood is the same power that our church leaders hold today.

After the Savior's resurrection, he visited the apostles and chose a man named Peter to be the prophet of the Church of Jesus Christ. Peter had two counselors, named James and John. They were like our First Presidency is today.

Peter was a wonderful leader, and the church grew very quickly. Missionaries preached the gospel in many cities, and thousands of people joined the church. They built church buildings to meet in each week, and they loved each other very much. They shared with each other, and no one was poor among them. Heavenly Father blessed them for keeping the commandments.

Scripture:

And I will give unto thee the keys of the kingdom of heaven: and whatsoever thou shalt bind on earth shall be bound in heaven: and whatsoever thou shalt loose on earth shall be loosed in heaven. (Matthew 16:19)

Visual Aid:
GAPK #235
Resurrected Jesus
speaks with the apostles

The apostles healed the sick

Scripture:

We believe in the same organization that existed in the Primitive Church, namely, apostles, prophets, pastors, teachers, evangelists, and so forth.
(Articles of Faith 1:6)

The priesthood is a special power given to men by Heavenly Father. When Jesus was on the earth, he held the priesthood. He used this power to heal people who were sick or injured. Jesus gave the priesthood power to his apostles, and they were also able to heal people. Two of the Savior's greatest apostles were Peter and John. One day they went to the temple, and outside the temple door was a man whose legs didn't work. Even when he was a child he hadn't been able to walk. Now he was a beggar, and he asked Peter for money so he wouldn't starve to death. Peter told the man that he didn't have any money, but that he would give him a greater gift. Then Peter told the man, "In the name of Jesus Christ, rise up and walk!"

Peter and John took the beggar by the hands and lifted him up, and immediately the man's legs were healed. He leaped into the air and walked into the temple, thanking Heavenly Father that he had been healed. All the people in the temple were amazed at what had happened. Our church leaders have that same priesthood power today. Righteous men hold the Melchizedek Priesthood, and they can use the priesthood to bless those in need.

Visual Aid:
GAPK #613
Administering to the sick

The Savior's church was taken from the earth

Many years after the Savior's resurrection, the Church of Jesus Christ began to fall apart. Some leaders began to change the gospel teachings, and many people stopped coming to Church. Wicked men killed the apostles, and soon there weren't enough people left to run the church. As these good men died, the priesthood power was lost, because only righteous men can hold the priesthood.

People began to create their own churches, using only parts of the Savior's teachings. They changed the sacrament and many other church teachings. They even pretended to have the priesthood power. Heavenly Father and Jesus were sad that the Church of Jesus Christ was no longer on the earth. For many centuries the Church didn't exist, and the world was filled with wickedness.

But Heavenly Father inspired men to form the United States of America. In this new country, the people believed in Jesus Christ. They loved to read the Bible, and they lived righteously. The time had come to restore the Church of Jesus Christ to the earth.

Scripture:

I was answered that I must join none of them, for they were all wrong; and the Personage who addressed me said that all their creeds were an abomination in his sight; that those professors were all corrupt; that "they draw near to me with their lips, but their hearts are far from me, they teach for doctrines the commandments of men, having a form of godliness, but they deny the power thereof." (Joseph Smith — History 1:19)

Visual Aid:
GAPK #240
Jesus the Christ

Chapter 2

I belong to The Church of Jesus Christ of Latter-day Saints

The Father and the Son visited Joseph Smith

Scripture:

For thus shall my church be called in the last days, even The Church of Jesus Christ of Latter-day Saints. (D&C 115:4)

Visual Aid:
GAPK #403
The First Vision

When the time came to restore the Church of Jesus Christ to the earth, Heavenly Father sent a strong, righteous spirit that had been specially chosen for this purpose. That person was Joseph Smith. He wasn't sent to a rich or well-known family. In fact, his parents were poor. But Heavenly Father knew they believed in the Bible and would raise Joseph the right way.

In the year 1820, when Joseph was fourteen, he lived in New York. All of his neighbors were talking about religion, but Joseph was confused about which church to join. He wanted to follow Heavenly Father, but none of the churches made sense to him. Then one night Joseph read a scripture in the Bible that said a person should pray if he has a question, and the answer would be given to him.

Joseph decided to try it. He went into a grove of trees to pray, and he received a wonderful visit from Heavenly Father and Jesus Christ. They told him that the Church of Jesus Christ was no longer on the earth, but that Joseph would help restore it. The church would have the same organization as the church that Jesus organized when he was on the earth. We are members of that church today.

Joseph Smith was visited by Angel Moroni

Three years after Joseph Smith was visited by Heavenly Father and Jesus Christ, he was visited by an angel named Moroni. He told Joseph about a special book that had been written on gold plates. This book told about the Nephites and Lamanites, who had lived long ago. Moroni told Joseph he should get the plates and translate them from the Nephite language into English. This book would be called the Book of Mormon, and the teachings in the book would help Joseph restore the Church of Jesus Christ.

Moroni told Joseph that the gold plates were buried in a hill, which is called the Hill Cumorah. Joseph went to the hill and found the plates in a stone box under a large rock. But Joseph wasn't quite ready to have the plates yet. He needed to get older and show that he would keep the commandments. Moroni told Joseph to come back to the Hill Cumorah each year.

After four years, Moroni finally let Joseph take the plates. Through the power of God, Joseph translated the plates, and the Book of Mormon was published. We are blessed to have the Book of Mormon to read today.

Scripture:

I give unto you my servant Joseph to be a presiding elder over all my church, to be a translator, a revelator, a seer, and prophet.
(D&C 124:125)

Visual Aids:
GAPK #404
Moroni appears to Joseph Smith
GAPK #406
Joseph receives the gold plates

The priesthood was restored to Joseph Smith

When Joseph Smith was translating the Book of Mormon, he came to a part about the importance of baptism. Joseph knew he had never been baptized, so he and his friend Oliver Cowdery went into the woods to pray about it. While they prayed, an angel named John the Baptist appeared. John the Baptist had baptized Jesus, and he held the priesthood power to baptize. The angel put his hands on the head of Joseph and then Oliver, and ordained them to the Aaronic Priesthood. This gave them the power to baptize. The two men quickly went to a nearby river, and Joseph first baptized Oliver, then Oliver baptized Joseph.

A few days later Joseph and Oliver received a special visit from Peter, James, and John, the men who had been the leaders of the church in Jerusalem after the Savior's resurrection. These men laid their hands on the heads of Joseph and Oliver, ordaining them to the Melchizedek Priesthood. This gave them the same power Peter, James and John had held when they led the Savior's church. Joseph now had the power to restore the Church of Jesus Christ to the earth.

Scripture:

Upon you my fellow servants, in the name of Messiah I confer the Priesthood of Aaron, which holds the keys of the ministering of angels, and of the gospel of repentance, and of baptism by immersion for the remission of sins; and this shall never be taken again from the earth, until the sons of Levi do offer again an offering unto the Lord in righteousness. (D&C 13:1)

Visual Aids:
GAPK #407
John the Baptist conferring the Aaronic Priesthood
GAPK # 408
Restoration of the Melchizedek Priesthood

The Church was restored on April 6, 1830

By the spring of 1830, ten years had passed since Joseph Smith had first received the visit from Heavenly Father and Jesus Christ. He had done many things in that time, such as translate the Book of Mormon and receive the priesthood from heavenly messengers.

During those years he had told many people that the Church of Jesus Christ would be restored. Finally on April 6, 1830, Joseph called for a meeting to be held at Peter Whitmer's farmhouse in Fayette, New York. Many people gathered at the farmhouse that day, and the church was officially organized according to the laws of the state of New York. The people accepted Joseph as the President of the Church, and then they took the sacrament. Also, those who had already been baptized were confirmed members of the church and received the gift of the Holy Ghost.

A special moment for Joseph happened later that afternoon when his parents were baptized. After his father's baptism, Joseph said, "Praise the Lord that I lived to see my own father baptized into the true Church of Jesus Christ!" Everyone was very happy that the Church had finally been restored to the earth.[1]

Scripture:

And this shall be our covenant—that we will walk in all the ordinances of the Lord. (D&C 36:4)

Visual Aid:
GAPK #401
The Prophet Joseph Smith

Chapter 3

I know
who I am

Heber J. Grant learned a good lesson

Scripture:

And if men come unto me I will show unto them their weakness. I give unto men weakness that they may be humble; and my grace is sufficient for all men that humble themselves before me; for if they humble themselves before me, and have faith in me, then will I make weak things become strong unto them. (Ether 12:27)

Visual Aid:
GAPK #512
Heber J. Grant

When Heber J. Grant was a young boy, he attended a Sacrament meeting where the man giving the talk couldn't speak very well. At first, young Heber laughed a little at the man, but as he listened to the man's words, he could feel the Holy Ghost very strongly. He knew the man had a testimony of the gospel, and Heber decided he wouldn't ever again judge anyone by their outward appearance. He knew that what matters isn't how a person dresses or talks, but whether the person has a good heart and is trying to do what is right. We are all children of God, and we don't want to hurt other people. We want to help them be the best they can be.

President Joseph F. Smith said it is wrong for children to make fun of each other, and it especially shouldn't be done by children who are members of the Church of Jesus Christ of Latter-day Saints. He said we should be kind to each other, because within each person is a wonderful spirit that is growing and becoming like our Heavenly Father. We all have weaknesses, but if we have faith in the Savior to help us, those weaknesses will become strengths to us, and help us return to live with Heavenly Father.

Wilford Woodruff's childhood accidents

The children of the Church have been saved by Heavenly Father for the last days. Because they were obedient before they were born, they were saved to come to earth at this time to help the Savior prepare for the Second Coming. But life isn't always easy. President Wilford Woodruff had many accidents as a child. At age three, he fell into a big pot of boiling water and was badly burned. Later, he fell from the top of a barn onto his face. Soon after, he fell down some stairs, breaking one of his arms. That same year, he fell from a porch and broke his other arm.

President Woodruff joined the Church as an adult, and even his baptism day was filled with danger. He said, "The day that I was baptized into the Church, my horse kicked the hat off my head. If the hoof had struck two inches lower, it would have killed me instantly." Ten minutes later, he began driving to his baptism in a sled pulled by two horses. On the way, the sled hit a rock. This threw President Woodruff forward between the horses. The frightened horses ran down the hill, dragging him under the sled. But he made it to his baptism. Despite his troubles, President Woodruff didn't complain. He did his best to serve the Lord, and became one of the greatest missionaries of all time.[2]

Scripture:

For verily I say unto you, blessed is he that keepeth my commandments, whether in life or in death; and he that is faithful in tribulation, the reward of the same is greater in the kingdom of heaven. (D&C 58:2)

Visual Aid:
GAPK#509
Wilford Woodruff

Scripture:

Wherefore, my beloved brethren, pray unto the Father with all the energy of heart, that ye may be filled with this love, which he hath bestowed upon all who are true followers of his Son, Jesus Christ; that ye may become the sons of God; that when he shall appear we shall be like him, for we shall see him as he is; that we may have this hope; that we may be purified even as he is pure. Amen.
(Moroni 7:48)

Visual Aid:
GAPK #320
 Moroni hides the gold plates in the Hill Cumorah

Moroni stayed true to the gospel

We are all children of God who can choose the right no matter what situation we are placed in. The prophet Moroni is a great example to us of keeping Heavenly Father's commandments. Moroni's father was named Mormon, and they were both leaders of the Nephites. But there was a great battle, and soon only 24 Nephites were still alive. The next day the battle continued, and Mormon was killed. At the end of the day, Moroni was the only Nephite left. He went into the forest and hid from the Lamanites, taking the gold plates with him.

Moroni was alone for many years, and he could have become very bitter and angry, but instead he still believed in Jesus Christ. He wrote on the gold plates that we should be filled with love and become like the Savior. At the end of his life, Moroni buried the gold plates in a stone box in the Hill Cumorah. Then many years later, he appeared to Joseph Smith and told him where to find the gold plates that Joseph translated into the Book of Mormon. We should be grateful that Moroni stayed true to the gospel throughout his life.

The musician who became a prophet

Everyone comes to earth with different talents. Some children are good at math, while others can sing really well. This is how Heavenly Father planned it. Since we each have our own set of talents, we can all serve in different ways.

As a young man, Howard W. Hunter didn't enjoy playing sports, but he really liked music. He took piano and violin lessons, and even played the drums. Later he taught himself to also play the clarinet and the trumpet. He and his friends formed a music band. They were very popular and played the music for many dances.

But President Hunter had another special talent. He had the gift of being humble. He didn't let his band's success make him think he was better than other people.

President Hunter kept this talent all his life. He liked to surprise people with kind words or good deeds if someone needed help. President Hunter was a great musician, but he was even greater at using his other gifts to bless the lives of many people.[3]

Scripture:

For all have not every gift given unto them; for there are many gifts, and to every man is given a gift by the Spirit of God.
(D&C 46:11)

Visual Aid:
GAPK #519
Howard W. Hunter

Chapter 4

I believe in the Savior Jesus Christ

Alma believed in the Savior

Scripture:

Now I say unto you, if this be the desire of your hearts, what have you against being baptized in the name of the Lord, as a witness before him that ye have entered into a covenant with him, that ye will serve him and keep his commandments, that he may pour out his Spirit more abundantly upon you? (Mosiah 18:10)

Visual Aid:
GAPK #309
Alma baptizes in the Waters of Mormon

There once was a wicked Nephite leader named King Noah. He didn't obey Heavenly Father's teachings. A prophet named Abinadi told King Noah he needed to repent and follow the teachings of the gospel, such as the Ten Commandments. But King Noah didn't repent, and he had Abinadi killed. But one person did believe Abinadi's words. His name was Alma, and he was one of the king's priests. King Noah tried to kill Alma, too, but Alma escaped.

Alma started teaching people about Jesus Christ, and soon many people had joined him at a secret meeting place. They all wanted to become members of the Savior's church. So Alma took them to a place called the Waters of Mormon. Alma baptized more than two hundred people into the Church that day.

The people were very happy, and they clapped their hands with joy. They thanked Heavenly Father for their blessings, and that they had been taught the gospel. They were grateful to be members of the Church.

Baptized in a bathtub

When a person has faith in Jesus Christ and agrees to keep the commandments, he or she can be baptized into the Church of Jesus Christ of Latter-day Saints. Spencer W. Kimball was so excited to be baptized that he just couldn't wait. He asked to be baptized on his eighth birthday.

Although there was a canal just a block away, someone suggested Spencer be baptized in a big metal container that the Kimball family used as a bathtub. It seemed like a good idea. That way everyone wouldn't have to walk down to the canal. So Spencer's father filled the tub with water, then baptized him in the tub.

Four years later when Spencer was ready to become a deacon, someone wondered if his baptism in a tub was okay. The person said Spencer's father had not gone down into the water too, as John the Baptist did when he baptized Jesus. Just to be safe, Spencer was baptized again, this time in the Union Canal. So President Kimball got to be baptized twice![4]

Scripture:

And it came to pass in those days, that Jesus came from Nazareth of Galilee, and was baptized of John in Jordan.
(Mark 1:9)

Visual Aid:
GAPK #517
Spencer W. Kimball

Scripture:

For behold, again I say unto you that if ye will enter in by the way, and receive the Holy Ghost, it will show unto you all things what ye should do. (2 Nephi 32:5)

Visual Aid:
GAPK #510
Lorenzo Snow

Lorenzo Snow was the oldest child in his family, and had his share of chores on the farm. He always did them quickly, and his parents were proud of him. But his real reason for being obedient was so he could get back to his favorite thing in the world — reading! He only attended one term of high school, but he had learned so much from his books that he was accepted to Oberlin College.

Lorenzo was a young man when he heard about the gospel, and he studied a long time before being baptized. Then after his baptism and confirmation he didn't immediately feel the Holy Ghost. He was disappointed and soon went into a field to pray.

President Snow later said, "I had no sooner opened my lips in an effort to pray, than I heard a sound, just above my head, like the rustling of silken robes, and immediately the Spirit of God descended upon me, filling me from the crown of my head to the soles of my feet, and oh, the joy and happiness I felt!"

President Snow said he could never deny that feeling of peace and joy. We can feel the Holy Ghost in our lives, too, as we keep the commandments.[5]

Primary is more important than hauling hay

Spencer W. Kimball had two older brothers who liked to tease him a lot. In the summer the three boys would work in the hay fields. The older boys would collect the hay with pitchforks, then toss it into the wagon and Spencer would tromp it down. The older boys purposely bothered Spencer. One would throw his hay on top of Spencer, knocking him down, then the other would add his load. They would laugh while Spencer angrily picked himself up. Sometimes he would even cry. But one day he got even with them.

When Spencer was young, Primary took place during the week. One hot afternoon, the boys heard the Primary bell ringing across the fields. Spencer told his brothers, "I've got to go to Primary," but they told him he had to stay and work.

Spencer then said, "If Pa were here he'd let me go to Primary." But his older brothers said, "Well, Pa is not here, and this is one time you're not going to Primary."

The brothers kept throwing hay until it had all piled in the center of the wagon. They called out, "Spencer, what's the matter with you up there?" There was no sound. They looked across the field and saw Spencer running as fast as his little legs would carry him. He was already halfway to the church! He knew he should be in Primary.[6]

Scripture:

If thou wilt do good, yea, and hold out faithful to the end, thou shalt be saved in the kingdom of God, which is the greatest of all the gifts of God; for there is no gift greater than the gift of salvation.
(D&C 6:13)

Visual Aid:
GAPK #517
Spencer W. Kimball

Chapter 5

The prophet speaks for the Savior

A living prophet guides the Church

President Gordon B. Hinckley was ordained the prophet in 1995. He is the fifteenth man to lead the Church of Jesus Christ of Latter-day Saints. When a prophet dies, the apostles meet and a new prophet is ordained. The member of the Quorum of the Twelve who has been an apostle for the longest time will be the next prophet.

When Lorenzo Snow found out that President Wilford Woodruff had died, he knew he would be the next president of the Church. He went to the Salt Lake Temple, where he pleaded with the Lord to tell him what to do. But an answer didn't come. So he walked though the temple, and Jesus Christ appeared to him. President Snow said the Savior stood about three feet above the floor, and it looked like he was standing on a plate of solid gold.

The Savior told President Snow that he would be the next person to lead the Church, and that he should go right ahead and reorganize the First Presidency at once.

The way the Savior chooses a prophet is a wonderful plan. There isn't an election, which could cause contention in the Church. Instead, everyone knows that the apostle who has served the longest will be the next prophet.

Scripture:

What I the Lord have spoken, I have spoken, and I excuse not myself; and though the heavens and the earth pass away, my word shall not pass away, but shall all be fulfilled, whether by mine own voice or by the voice of my servants, it is the same. (D&C 1:38)

Visual Aids:
GAPK #520
Gordon B. Hinckley
GAPK # 510
Lorenzo Snow

The Book of Mormon is a blessing

As members of the Church we can read from a very special book — The Book of Mormon. It tells wonderful stories about a family who lived many years ago. A man named Lehi and his family lived in the city of Jerusalem. Heavenly Father told Lehi the city was going to be destroyed. Lehi's family left the city and traveled many days. Then they built a boat and sailed across the ocean to the American continent.

Lehi's son Nephi became a great prophet and wrote many important things that are in the Book of Mormon. The book also tells about the Savior's visit to these people after he was resurrected, and the Book of Mormon gives us many important teachings about how to become like the Savior.

The prophets have asked us to each read from the scriptures for at least ten minutes a day. By keeping this commandment we will be blessed in many ways. If we are faithful, we will be happier and be nicer to other people. Most importantly, we will have the Holy Ghost with us and be on the path to living with Heavenly Father again.

Scripture:

And moreover, I would desire that ye should consider on the blessed and happy state of those that keep the commandments of God. For behold, they are blessed in all things, both temporal and spiritual; and if they hold out faithful to the end they are received into heaven. (Mosiah 2:41)

Visual Aids:
GAPK #301
Lehi's family leaving Jerusalem
GAPK #304
Lehi and his family arrive in the Promised Land

The prophet speaks at General Conference

Scripture:

For his word ye shall receive, as if from mine own mouth, in all patience and faith. (D&C 21:5)

Visual Aid:
GAPK #608
Christ and children from around the world

We are blessed to have a living prophet on the earth. He gives us the messages that Heavenly Father wants us to hear. The prophet speaks at meetings many times during the year, but every six months the Church holds very special meetings called General Conference.

These meetings are held in the Conference Center in Salt Lake City, Utah. This is when the prophet, the twelve apostles, and other Church leaders speak to all of the members of the Church. General Conference is held the first weekend of April and then again the first weekend of October.

Since most church members live far from Salt Lake City, the Church shows the conference meetings on television, and also broadcasts them by satellite across the world in many languages.

Watching General Conference and then reading those messages in the Church magazines the next month can strengthen our testimonies of what the prophet and apostles have taught us to do in life.

28

The apostles bear testimony of Jesus

When Jesus lived on the earth, he called twelve men to be the leaders of the Church. They were known as the apostles. Just like in the Savior's time, we also have twelve apostles to help the prophet lead the Church. These men are special witnesses of the Savior, and they share their testimonies with people all over the world.

After he became the prophet, Heber J. Grant received a vision that showed him how he had been chosen to be an apostle. In the vision, he saw a meeting being held in the Spirit World. The Savior and the Prophet Joseph Smith were in the meeting, along with Heber's father, Jedediah Grant, who had been an apostle himself before dying at a young age.

At the time of the meeting, an apostle had died, and a new one needed to be chosen. During the meeting the Prophet Joseph Smith and Heber's father both mentioned Heber as being worthy, and asked the Savior that Heber be called as an apostle. The Savior agreed, and a revelation was given to President John Taylor, who called Heber to become the newest apostle.[7]

Scripture:

The twelve traveling councilors are called to be the Twelve Apostles, or special witnesses of the name of Christ in all the world — thus differing from other officers in the church in the duties of their calling.
(D&C 107:23)

Visual Aid:

GAPK #512
Heber J. Grant

Chapter 6

I know
God's plan

Scripture:

For behold, this is my work and my glory—to bring to pass the immortality and eternal life of man. (Moses 1:39)

Our life on earth is part of Heavenly Father's plan for us to become like him. We began as spirits, living with Heavenly Father in heaven. The next step in the plan was to come to earth, so we could have physical bodies.

When we die, our body and spirit separate. Our body is buried in the ground, but our spirit will go to the Spirit World. The Spirit World has two parts. If we have been good, we will go to a place in the Spirit World called Paradise. If we have been wicked, we will go to a place called Spirit Prison.

After the Second Coming, when the Savior comes to earth again, we will be resurrected. To be resurrected means to have our body and spirit come together again. After we are resurrected, we won't ever get sick, and any injuries or scars we had on our bodies will be gone. We will be like Heavenly Father and Jesus, who have resurrected bodies.

Once we are resurrected, we will be assigned to live forever in a kingdom. There are three different kingdoms. The most wicked people will go the Telestial Kingdom.

People who were nice, but that didn't believe in Jesus, will live in the Terrestrial Kingdom. And finally, those who were righteous will live forever in the Celestial Kingdom with Heavenly Father and Jesus.

Visual Aid:
GAPK #238
The Second Coming

Joseph Smith saved the snakes

Heavenly Father and Jesus created the earth and all forms of life, and they are happy when we treat animals with kindness. A good example of this happened in the 1830s, when Joseph Smith led a group of men from Ohio to Missouri. They called themselves Zion's Camp, and they were traveling to help protect the Saints there. As they camped in the wilderness each night, many snakes would sneak into their tents to get warm. This frightened some of the men. They were afraid of being bitten, and they would kill the snakes.

This made Joseph unhappy, and he told the men not to hurt the snakes. He said rather than kill them, they should quietly carry the snakes from their tents on sticks. Joseph promised the men that if they would do this, none of them would be bitten. Joseph told the men it was their duty to set an example of peace.

The men in the camp followed the prophet's advice, and none of the men were bitten during their journey. Heavenly Father is happy when we treat the earth and all living things with respect.[8]

Scripture:

Behold, I am Jesus Christ the Son of God. I created the heavens and the earth, and all things that in them are. I was with the Father from the beginning. *(3 Nephi 9:15)*

Visual Aid:
GAPK #401
The Prophet Joseph Smith

For behold, this life is the time for men to prepare to meet God; yea, behold the day of this life is the day for men to perform their labors. (Alma 34:32)

Visual Aids:
GAPK #514
David O. McKay
GAPK #239
The Resurrected Jesus Christ

A vision of the Savior's celestial city

President David O. McKay once had a vision that showed him the future home of those who follow the Savior. President McKay saw a beautiful white city with fruit-filled trees and beautiful flowers. He also saw many people approaching the city. Each person wore white clothing, and everyone was looking at a heavenly person who stood in the center of the city. President McKay knew it was Jesus Christ. President McKay said, "The city was his. It was the City Eternal; and the people following him were to live there in peace and eternal happiness."

President McKay wanted to know how these people had earned the right to live in the Savior's city. He then said, "As if the Savior read my thoughts, he answered by pointing to a semicircle that appeared above us, on which were written in gold the words: 'These Are They Who Have Overcome The World—Who Have Truly Been Born Again!'" When we are baptized and receive the Holy Ghost, it is like we are born again. We leave behind our old sins and start clean and new. If we choose to follow the Savior and obey the commandments the rest of our lives, we can live with him again.[9]

Nephi chose to be a peacemaker

Heavenly Father sends us to earth to see how we will choose between right and wrong. To help us learn and grow, we are sent as part of a family.

Many of us have brothers and sisters, and sometimes it isn't easy to get along. Satan wants us to fight and make each other angry, but Heavenly Father wants us to be kind to each other.

The prophet Nephi faced that situation when he was a boy. Nephi believed the teachings of his father Lehi, and he knew the gospel was true. But Nephi's older brothers didn't believe their father. They were named Laman and Lemuel, and they were mean to Nephi. They made fun of him for believing in the Savior. They hit him with a stick, and one time they even tied him up for three days.

Nephi chose not to fight back or lose his temper. Instead, he told his brothers he hoped they would change and believe the gospel plan. They never did, but Nephi was protected. One time when Laman and Lemuel were being wicked, the Lord told Nephi to touch his brothers. When he touched them, they felt a shock. They knew the Lord was with him.

Scripture:

Wherefore, I, Nephi, did strive to keep the commandments of the Lord, and I did exhort my brethren to faithfulness and diligence.
(1 Nephi 17:15)

Visual Aid:
GAPK #303
Nephi and his
rebellious brothers

Chapter 7

I will follow Him in faith

Alma taught the right way to pray

Ye must pour out your souls in your closets, and your secret places, and in your wilderness. Yea, and when you do not cry unto the Lord, let your hearts be full, drawn out in prayer unto him continually for your welfare, and also for the welfare of those who are around you. (Alma 34:26-27)

Visual Aid:
GAPK #605
A young boy praying

The Book of Mormon tells us about a group of people called the Zoramites. They had once been strong members of the Church, but they began to do wicked things. The prophet Alma felt he should visit them.

When he came to their city, he was very surprised. He found the people talked about Heavenly Father only one day a week. On that day, they would gather at their church. In the middle of the church they had built a tower, and each person would take a turn standing on the tower and saying the exact same prayer that everyone else said. In their prayer they said they didn't believe in Jesus Christ.

Alma was very sad, so he and his friends tried to teach the Zoramites the right way to pray. They taught the people to pray as if they are talking directly to Heavenly Father. The prophets teach us that we can pray anytime and anywhere. If we are in danger or need help in school, we can even pray in our minds. Heavenly Father will hear our prayers.

Praying is one of the most important things we can do. When we talk with Heavenly Father, we become spiritually stronger and more able to resist temptation.

A baby is brought back to life

In the year 1921 President David O. McKay was a young apostle. He visited the island of Samoa and blessed the land and the village for the preaching of the gospel.

While he was there a man approached President McKay and asked if he could give a blessing to his sister's baby boy, who was very sick. They rushed to the sister's house, but they didn't make it in time. The baby had already died and was starting to turn black. But President McKay said a prayer in his heart, and was prompted to bless the baby. He put his hands on the baby's head. By using the holy priesthood he blessed the baby to come back to life. Everyone watched as the child began to breath again. He returned to perfect health.

Thirty-three years later, President McKay received a letter from a man who had been there that day. He told President McKay that the young baby had grown up to be a healthy man and had moved to New Zealand, where he was raising a family. Miracles still happen in the church today.[10]

Scripture:

I came unto my own, and mine own received me not; but unto as many as received me gave I power to do many miracles, and to become the sons of God; and even unto them that believed on my name gave I power to obtain eternal life. (D&C 45:8)

Visual Aid:
GAPK #514
David O. McKay

We can be an example to our family

Scripture:

Angels speak by the power of the Holy Ghost; wherefore, they speak the words of Christ. Wherefore, I said unto you, feast upon the words of Christ; for behold, the words of Christ will tell you all things what ye should do. (2 Nephi 32:3)

Visual Aid:
GAPK #519
Howard W. Hunter

We show faith when we obey Heavenly Father's commandments. When we trust in the Lord, we can overcome many challenges.

When President Howard W. Hunter was a boy, he faced a hard challenge when he turned eight years old. Howard's father wasn't a church member, and he didn't want Howard to join the Church, either. But Howard prayed every night that his father would change his mind and let him be baptized.

Howard went to church every week for many years, and Howard really wanted to become a deacon and pass the sacrament. But he still wasn't a member of the Church. Howard's father saw that his son had great faith, and finally when Howard was twelve years old, his father allowed him to be baptized.

Many years later, Howard's father did join the Church, and he thanked Howard for being a good example to him. Then on Howard's 46th birthday, he received a special surprise. He was in a meeting at the temple when his parents came into the room dressed in white. That day they were sealed together as an eternal family.[11]

The Benson family's spiritual harvest

In the early days of the church, there weren't many young men available to serve missions, so husbands and fathers would be called to serve. When President Ezra Taft Benson was twelve years old, his father, George Benson, was called to serve a mission in the Midwestern United States.

There were seven children in the Benson home when he left, and an eighth would soon be born. Ezra, as the oldest son, had to carry much of the responsibility for the farm. One of President Benson's favorite memories was when the family sat at the kitchen table and listened to their mother read George's weekly missionary letters.

President Benson later said, "There came into our home a spirit of missionary work that never left." All eleven Benson children later served missions, and they were grateful for the example of their father, who followed the Savior, even when it seemed difficult. But the family knew they were blessed in taking care of the farm during George's mission, and they received a great spiritual harvest as well.[12]

Scripture:

And he said unto the children of men: Follow thou me. Wherefore, my beloved brethren, can we follow Jesus save we shall be willing to keep the commandments of the Father? (2 Nephi 31:10)

Visual Aid:
GAPK #518
Ezra Taft Benson

Chapter 8

I will honor His name

We follow the Savior through baptism

Scripture:

And as many as repent and are baptized in my name, which is Jesus Christ, and endure to the end, the same shall be saved. (D&C 18:22)

The most important step we can make is to choose to be baptized into the Church of Jesus Christ of Latter-day Saints. Baptism opens the way to the Celestial Kingdom. The Savior set an example for us by being baptized. He knew baptism is the way back to heaven.

In the Book of Mormon, the prophet Nephi compares baptism to a gate leading to heaven. Picture in your mind the Celestial Kingdom as a beautiful white home that is surrounded by a tall white fence. The fence has only one opening—a sparkling gate that lets us onto a path to the home. If we never enter the gate, we won't be able to live in the Celestial Kingdom.

Once we are baptized, we have entered the gate, but we still must obey Heavenly Father the rest of our lives if we are going to reach the Celestial Kingdom. We can stay on the path to heaven by attending church and keeping the commandments.

If we stay on the right path, at the end of our lives we will find ourselves at the door to that beautiful white home, and Heavenly Father will welcome us in!

Visual Aids:
GAPK #208
John the Baptist baptizing Jesus
GAPK #601
Baptism

The sacrament reminds us of the Savior

Just before Jesus was crucified, he held a special dinner with his apostles called the Last Supper. The Savior knew he was going to die, and he wanted the members of the church to always remember him. So he taught his apostles an ordinance called the sacrament.

First, Jesus took some bread and blessed it. He told his apostles that the bread represented his body, and the sacrifice he was making to redeem us from our sins.

Next, Jesus took a cup of wine and blessed it, telling his apostles that it represented the blood he would shed for us in the Garden of Gethsemane and on the cross. Jesus gave his life for us so that we could live again with Heavenly Father.

After his resurrection, Jesus visited the Nephites in America. He taught them about the sacrament, too.

When Joseph Smith restored the Church, the sacrament was given during the first meeting. Today, Sacrament Meeting is the most important meeting in the church. As we take the sacrament, we renew our baptismal covenants and promise to keep the Lord's commandments and always remember him.

Scripture:

Therefore, I would that ye should behold that the Lord did truly teach the people, for the space of three days; and after that he did show himself unto them oft, and did break bread oft, and bless it, and give it unto them.
(3 Nephi 26:13)

Visual Aid:
GAPK #225
The Last Supper

45

Primary children should use clean language

Thou shalt not take the name of the Lord thy God in vain; for the Lord will not hold him guiltless that taketh his name in vain. (Exodus 20:7)

Visual Aid:
GAPK #517
Spencer W. Kimball

President Spencer W. Kimball truly loved Heavenly Father and Jesus. One day he was in the hospital for an operation, and was being wheeled out of the operating room and back to his hospital bed.

The man pushing him stumbled, and from the man's mouth came some very bad words, including the name of Jesus being used as a swear word.

President Kimball was only half-awake, but he was sad to hear the Savior's name being used in the wrong way. He said to the man, "Please don't say that! That is my Lord!" There was a long silence, then the attendant whispered, "I am sorry."

Our church leaders have told us to not swear or tell dirty jokes. We can be an example to our friends and family by not using mean or dirty words. We should always use the names of Heavenly Father and Jesus reverently. If we do, we will be happier and have the Holy Ghost with us.[13]

Primary has been taught for 125 years

The first Primary meeting was held on August 25, 1878, in Farmington, Utah, a few miles north of Salt Lake City. It was a great success. Sister Aurelia Spencer Rogers stood at the entrance of the Farmington, Utah, meetinghouse and greeted 224 boys and girls. They sang songs and heard a short lesson from Sister Rogers.

Sister Rogers organized the Primary, with President John Taylor's approval, because she had noticed the rough and careless behavior of the boys in her neighborhood. She had wondered, "What will our girls do for good husbands, if this state of things continues?"

She decided to begin an organization for boys that could make them become better men and be obedient to Heavenly Father's commandments.

Girls were invited to Primary because Sister Rogers knew the boys would need help with the singing. During the next few years, Primary was started in almost every LDS settlement. This is the 125th year since the Primary began. It has a special place in the Church, because this is where most children first learn about Jesus Christ.[14]

Scripture:

There is no other name given whereby salvation cometh; therefore, I would that ye should take upon you the name of Christ, all you that have entered into the covenant with God that ye should be obedient unto the end of your lives. (Mosiah 5:8)

Visual Aid:
GAPK #607
Young girl speaking at church

Chapter 9

I will do what is right

"Harold, don't go over there."

Scripture:

And by the power of the Holy Ghost ye may know the truth of all things. (Moroni 10:5)

Visual Aid:
GAPK # 516
Harold B. Lee

As a little boy, President Harold B. Lee had his first experience with the promptings of the Holy Ghost. He was out on a farm playing when he saw over the fence in the neighbor's yard some old buildings where the roofs were caving in and the walls were rotting. He thought it would be a great place to explore, so he went to the fence and started to climb through.

Then he heard a voice say, "Harold, don't go over there." He looked around to see who had said that to him, but there was no one in sight. He realized he had been warned by the Holy Ghost of an unseen danger.

President Lee later said, "Whether there was a nest of rattlesnakes over there or whether the rotting timbers would fall on me and crush me, I don't know. But from that time on, I accepted without question the fact that we can hear voices from the unseen world." He knew Heavenly Father was watching over him and protecting him.[15]

The Savior is our best friend

During our lives, we make many friends. Some live in our neighborhood, or we get to know them at school. Friends can make our lives so much more enjoyable.

It is important, though, to choose friends who want to do what is right. A friend who wants us to do things that are wrong isn't really our friend, and will probably lead us into trouble.

There is one person who will always be there for us, no matter what. That is the Savior Jesus Christ. Jesus wants us to do what is right so that we can return and live with Heavenly Father. By studying his life and following his teachings, we can grow close to him. Through the Holy Ghost, we can feel his love for us.

President Ezra Taft Benson told us that becoming true friends with the Savior is the key to success in life. He said, "The only true test of greatness, blessedness, and joyfulness is how close a life can come to being like the Master, Jesus Christ. He is the right way, the full truth, and the abundant life."

We will be blessed as we honor and love the Savior, and as we choose friends who love him, too.[16]

Scripture:

Therefore, all things whatsoever ye would that men should do to you, do ye even so to them, for that is the law and the prophets. (3 Nephi 14:12)

Visual Aid:
GAPK #240
The Savior Jesus Christ

Pigs are sometimes like bad habits

I say unto you, can ye look up to God at that day with a pure heart and clean hands? I say unto you, can you look up, having the image of God engraven upon your countenances? (Alma 5:19)

Visual Aid:
GAPK #517
Spencer W. Kimball

As a young boy, Spencer W. Kimball grew up in the small farming town of Thatcher, Arizona. When he was a young boy, it was his job to feed the family's pigs. If his father heard the pigs squealing he would ask Spencer, "Haven't you fed your pigs yet?"

It seemed to Spencer those pigs never got full. Years later he joked that carrying all those heavy cans of food to the pigs had stunted his growth and made him short.

Spencer's pigs were always getting loose. No matter how many holes Spencer plugged in the wire fence, the pigs would find new ones. When he found a pig missing, Spencer would run next door and would usually find the pig in the neighbor's garden eating their vegetables. The neighbors didn't like that very much. Then when Spencer finally would get the pig home, the pig never seemed able to squeeze back through the hole where it got out.

Those pigs are a lot like bad habits and sins. If we let bad thoughts get loose in our mind, they can cause us a lot of trouble. But if we control them and keep our mind and body clean and pure, we can live happy, righteous lives.[17]

Hold to the Iron Rod

When the prophet Lehi lived in Jerusalem, the Lord showed him a special dream. Lehi saw the Tree of Life. It was filled with delicious fruit. Those who reached the tree and ate the fruit would receive eternal life.

But reaching the tree wasn't easy. Lehi saw many people get lost and wander off in strange directions. He saw other people get tempted away by people who lived in a big building that was filled with riches.

Lehi saw that the only way to reach the Tree of Life was to hold onto a metal railing along a narrow path. The railing was called the Iron Rod. If people didn't hold onto the Iron Rod, they would fall off into a river. Sometimes mists of darkness would come, and if the people weren't holding onto the Iron Rod, they would wander off the path.

The Book of Mormon says the Iron Rod is a symbol for the scriptures. If we study the scriptures each day, we will stay on the path that leads back to the Celestial Kingdom. We won't be distracted by the temptations of the world if we hold onto the Iron Rod.

Scripture:

And it came to pass that I beheld others pressing forward, and they came forth and caught hold of the end of the rod of iron; and they did press forward through the mist of darkness, clinging to the rod of iron, even until they did come forth and partake of the fruit of the tree. (1 Nephi 8:24)

Visual Aid:
GAPK #326
The Bible and Book of Mormon

Chapter 10

I will follow His light

Eleven pieces of licorice

Scripture:

And as I have prayed among you even so shall ye pray in my church, among my people who do repent and are baptized in my name. Behold I am the light; I have set an example for you. (3 Nephi 18:16)

Visual Aid:
GAPK #519
Howard W. Hunter

As an apostle, President Howard W. Hunter traveled all over the world. On one trip, he and his wife were waiting for a bus to arrive. As they waited, they spotted a small store nearby. They went into the store, and President Hunter saw that a piece of licorice only cost one penny.

President Hunter went to the store counter, picked out several pieces of licorice, and then paid the clerk ten pennies. Then he and his wife hurried back to catch the bus. President Hunter gave out the licorice to some people they were traveling with, then he suddenly realized he had miscounted. He had ended up with eleven pieces, instead of the ten pieces he had paid for! Most people would have overlooked the small error, but not President Hunter. He hurried back to the store, explained the problem to the surprised clerk, and paid the extra penny.

He barely made it back to the bus stop in time, but those who knew President Hunter were sure he would have missed the bus to make sure he had paid for every piece of licorice. President Hunter was a man who followed the Savior in everything he did, especially in being honest. Jesus is our greatest example, and he taught that honesty is the best way.[18]

Joseph Smith silenced the wicked guards

In 1838, Joseph Smith and his friends were captured by wicked men and held unjustly in a jail in Richmond, Missouri. He was forced to lay on a wooden floor and wear chains. There were guards watching him and his friends, and long past midnight the guards used swear words and talked about the terrible things they had done to members of the Church.

Finally Joseph had heard enough. Even though he was in chains and the guards had guns, Joseph arose to his feet and spoke in a voice like a roaring lion, saying, "Silence! In the name of Jesus Christ I rebuke you, and command you to be still. I will not live another minute and hear such language. Cease such talk, or you or I will die this instant!"

The apostle Parley P. Pratt was there, and he said that when Joseph finished speaking, the prophet stood there calmly, as dignified as an angel.

Parley said the guards nervously dropped their guns to the ground and crawled into a corner of the room. They begged Joseph to forgive them and remained quiet until the next guards came. They knew Joseph had the power of God with him.[19]

Scripture:

For the word of the Lord is truth, and whatsoever is truth is light, and whatsoever is light is Spirit, even the Spirit of Jesus Christ. (D&C 84:45)

Visual Aid:
GAPK #401
The Prophet Joseph Smith

Family Home Evening on national TV

Scripture:

Therefore, hold up your light that it may shine unto the world. Behold I am the light which ye shall hold up—that which ye have seen me do. Behold ye see that I have prayed unto the Father, and ye all have witnessed.
(3 Nephi 18:24)

Visual Aid:
GAPK #518
Ezra Taft Benson

President Ezra Taft Benson was always a good example to people who weren't members of the Church. In the 1950s, long before he served as the president of the Church, President Benson was the U.S. Secretary of Agriculture, a very important position in the United States government. He worked closely with Dwight D. Eisenhower, who was the president of the United States.

President Benson convinced President Eisenhower to begin each of their meetings with a prayer, and he never swore or drank alcohol like many of the men he worked with. President Benson and his family were good examples of how members of the church should live. Many national magazines and newspapers printed nice stories about the Church because of them.

The Bensons even had a TV news program come to their home to show Family Home Evening to the whole nation! The Bensons started with family prayer, then they sang together and had a short lesson. After the show, people across the United States wrote letters, thanking the Bensons for showing them how to strengthen their own families. As we follow the Savior and set a good example, other people will respect us and know we want to do what is right.[20]

Noah's family was safe in the ark

Adam and Eve were the first people on the earth. They had many children, and after many centuries, there were millions of people on the earth. But there were more wicked people than righteous people. The prophets told the people to repent, but they wouldn't listen. They just became more wicked.

Heavenly Father was unhappy with how the people were acting. He told his prophet Noah that the time had come to clean the earth of the wicked people. He told Noah to build a giant boat, called an ark, that would hold many animals. The Lord told Noah to warn the people that if they didn't repent and live righteously, the Lord would cause it to rain for forty days and forty nights. The entire earth would be flooded.

Noah warned the people to repent, but they just laughed at him. They thought he was crazy to build an ark. But when the ark was finished and all the animals had been gathered into it, Noah and his family shut the door. Then it started to rain. The Lord fulfilled his promise. The wicked people were killed, but Noah's family was safe. As we follow the Savior's light, we will be protected, too.

Scripture:

The Lord is my light and my salvation; whom shall I fear? The Lord is the strength of my life; of whom shall I be afraid? (Psalm 27:1)

Visual Aid:
GAPK #103
Noah and the Ark

Chapter 11

I will follow the teachings of the prophets

Preaching to the milk cows

When the prophet speaks at General Conference, he gives important messages that will help us in our lives. It is important that we read and remember what the prophet teaches us. President Spencer W. Kimball found ways to do that when he did chores as a young boy. His family lived on a farm, and when he was nine years old, it was his job to milk the cows. It was usually a boring job, and sometimes Spencer practiced squirting milk into the mouths the cats that gathered around at milking time.

Other times, Spencer would practice learning the Articles of Faith and the Ten Commandments as he squirted milk into the pail. He also would sing Church songs to the cows. On a one-legged stool, with his head resting against the cow's hip, he memorized most of the songs in the hymn book from sheets of paper on which he had copied them. Spencer learned that during even the most boring times, there are chances to practice songs and learn the teachings of the prophets, even if you are only preaching to the cows.[21]

Sunday can be a special day

Sunday is a very special day to Heavenly Father. He wants us to attend church on Sunday, and make it a day to remember the Savior. The prophets have given us ideas of what to do on Sunday to keep it holy. President Spencer W. Kimball said we may want to read the scriptures and Church magazines on Sunday, and write in our journals. We could also write letters to relatives, friends or missionaries. Some families sing Church songs together and talk about what they learned in church. Sunday is also a good day to visit people who are sick or lonely.

President Gordon B. Hinckley has asked us not to shop on Sunday. He said, "Nobody needs to shop on the Sabbath. You can buy enough meat on Saturday to get through Sunday. You can buy enough milk on Saturday to get through Sunday. You certainly do not need to buy clothing on Sunday nor furniture nor anything of that kind. Keep the Sabbath day holy." As we follow the prophets, we will be blessed and feel closer to Heavenly Father.[22]

Scripture:

And now, behold, two hundred years had passed away, and the people of Nephi had waxed strong in the land. They observed to keep the law of Moses and the sabbath day holy unto the Lord. (Jarom 1:5)

Visual Aid:
GAPK #617
Girl reading the scriptures

We should obey the Word of Wisdom

And all saints who remember to keep and do these sayings, walking in obedience to the commandments, shall receive health in their navel and marrow to their bones. (D&C 89:18)

We have been taught by the leaders of the Church to avoid taking into our bodies things that will harm us. Some of the things we shouldn't do is drink alcohol, smoke or chew tobacco, or take drugs.

Members of the Church are among the healthiest people in the world, because we obey the Word of Wisdom, which is a revelation from the Lord that tells us how to have a healthy life.

Joseph Smith received the Word of Wisdom soon after the Church began. Joseph would hold special meetings for the leaders called the School of the Prophets. The men would meet in a small room, and the first thing the men would do was light their pipes or chew on big chunks of tobacco. When the prophet entered the room to teach the men, he would find himself in a cloud of tobacco smoke.

This bothered Joseph. It also bothered his wife Emma, who had to clean the tobacco juice off the floor. Joseph finally asked the Lord whether the men should use tobacco. The Lord answered his question by giving Joseph the revelation known as the Word of Wisdom that we still follow in the Church today.[23]

The Savior wants me to dress nicely

The prophets have taught us that we should dress nicely. Many famous people today don't dress the way they should. They wear clothes that show too much of their bodies. Many people, even members of the Church, try to copy the way these famous people dress. This isn't what the Savior wants us to do. He wants us to be modest, meaning that we keep our bodies covered. This includes what we wear to school, as well as our swimsuits.

The reason why the Savior is concerned about what we wear is that our body is like a temple. It covers our spirit. When we worry too much about our clothing, we sometimes forget to remember the Church and the gospel teachings.

President Gordon B. Hinckley has told both the boys and the girls of the Church to be careful in what they wear. He has also asked us to not get tattoos or pierce our bodies. He said one pair of earrings for girls is enough, and that boys shouldn't wear them. As we follow the prophet's teachings, we will be blessed.[24]

Scripture:

There began to be among them those who were lifted up in pride, such as the wearing of costly apparel, and all manner of fine pearls, and of the fine things of the world.
(4 Nephi 1:24)

Visual Aids:
GAPK #240
Jesus the Christ
GAPK #520
Gordon B. Hinckley

Chapter 12

His truth
I will proclaim

The truth will burn in our hearts

Scripture:

Yea, behold, I will tell you to your mind and in your heart, by the Holy Ghost, which shall come upon you and which shall dwell in your heart. (D&C 8:2)

Visual Aid:
GAPK #602
The gift of the Holy Ghost

The Savior has promised a special gift for members of his Church. This is the gift of the Holy Ghost. Soon after a person is baptized, men who hold the priesthood gather around the person and place their hands on the person's head. Then one of the men gives a special blessing that confirms the person a member of the Church, and also gives them the gift of the Holy Ghost.

The Holy Ghost is a powerful spirit who has a special assignment. He lets people know the gospel is true. When we receive the gift of the Holy Ghost, this means the Holy Ghost will be there to always help us.

When we share our testimony with others, sometimes we will feel a very strong feeling in our chest, like it is burning. This is the Holy Ghost letting us know that the things we are talking about are true. Sometimes people cry when they bear their testimonies. But they aren't sad. They are happy, because they know that Jesus lives and that the Church is true.

When we tell other people about the Church, the Holy Ghost can touch their hearts, too.

I can share the gospel with others

Members of the Church don't have to wait until they are called as missionaries to share the gospel with other people. Many people have learned about the gospel through the example of young boys and girls who are proud to be members of the Church and who are living the way they should. This helps them prepare to serve as missionaries someday.

The prophets have asked that every worthy young man should serve a mission for the church when he turns nineteen years of age. That should be the goal of every young man, and he should discuss with his family about saving money to pay for his mission.

Young women who reach the age of twenty-one and aren't married are also able to serve as missionaries. Many older members of the Church also serve missions when they retire from their jobs.

Heavenly Father is always happy when someone decides to serve a mission. He has promised us great blessings in heaven for sharing the gospel and bringing others into the Church.

Scripture:

Therefore, go ye into all the world; and unto whatsoever place ye cannot go ye shall send, that the testimony may go from you into all the world unto every creature. (D&C 84:62)

Visual Aid:
GAPK #612
Missionaries teach the gospel

True blue, through and through

Scripture:

Let no man despise thy youth; but be thou an example of the believers, in word, in conversation, in charity, in spirit, in faith, in purity. (1 Timothy 4:12)

Visual Aid:
GAPK #511
Joseph F. Smith

It is possible to develop a strong testimony at a young age. Such was the case with President Joseph F. Smith. He served a mission in Hawaii when he was just fifteen years old.

When Joseph was on the way home from his mission, he joined a wagon train traveling from California to Utah. Some people didn't like members of our church. One day, several rough-looking men rode up to the camp on horseback. These men said they would hurt or even kill any Mormons they saw.

When the men arrived, Joseph was away from the camp gathering wood for the fire. He returned to see that the members of his camp were hiding out of sight in the bushes down by the creek. When he saw them hiding, he thought, "Shall I run from these fellows? Why should I fear them?"

With that he marched up and dropped an armful of wood by the campfire. One of the men waved a pistol in the air and said more bad things about the Mormons. Then in a loud voice he said to Joseph, "Are you a Mormon?"

Joseph turned to him and answered, "Yes, siree; dyed in the wool; true blue, through and through." At that, the rough-looking man grabbed him by the hand and said, "Shake my hand, young fellow, I am glad to see a man that stands up for his convictions."[25]

Glorious days await members of the Church

The Church of Jesus Christ of Latter-day Saints has a great future. The prophets have told us that the Church will continue to grow, and the gospel will be taken to every part of the earth.

The Church is the way Heavenly Father teaches his children the gospel. The Church brings happiness to those who follow the Savior, and in our classes we learn how to become like our Heavenly Father.

Someday the members of the Church will build a wonderful city in Jackson County, Missouri. This city will be called New Jerusalem, and members of the church will gather there. It will be a city filled with peace and harmony. Soon after, the Savior will return to earth, and when he comes again, one thousand years of peace will begin. This time will be called the Millennium.

By being active in the church throughout our lives, we will see glorious events take place. But most importantly, we will be blessed and earn a place in the Celestial Kingdom. We should always be grateful that we are members of the Savior's church.

Scripture:

Yea, and are willing to mourn with those that mourn; yea, and comfort those that stand in need of comfort, and to stand as witnesses of God at all times and in all things, and in all places that ye may be in, even until death, that ye may be redeemed of God, and be numbered with those of the first resurrection, that ye may have eternal life. (Mosiah 18:9)

Visual Aid:
GAPK #238
The Second Coming

References

1. Lucy Mack Smith. *History of Joseph Smith by His Mother*, p. 188.

2. Matthias F. Cowley. *Wilford Woodruff—His Life and Labors*, p. 8-10.

3. "President Howard W. Hunter," *Ensign*, April 1995, p. 9.

4. Kimball, Edward L., and Andrew E. Kimball, Jr. *Spencer W. Kimball*. Salt Lake City, Utah: Bookcraft, 1977, p. 27-28.

5. Smith, Eliza R. Snow. *Biography and Family Record of Lorenzo Snow*. Salt Lake City, Utah: Deseret News Company, 1884, p. 2, 8.

6. Kimball, Edward L., and Andrew E. Kimball, Jr. *Spencer W. Kimball*. Salt Lake City, Utah: Bookcraft, 1977, p. 32.

7. Grant, Heber J. *Gospel Standards*. Compiled by G. Homer Durham. Salt Lake City: 1943, p. 195.

8. Cowley, Matthias F. *Cowley's Talks on Doctrine*, Chattanooga, Tenn., Ben. E. Rich, 1902, p. 193-194.

9. Middlemiss, Claire. *Cherished Experiences of David O. McKay*, 1970, p. 101-102.

10. Middlemiss, Claire. *Cherished Experiences of David O. McKay*, 1970, p. 162.

11. "President Howard W. Hunter," *Ensign*, April 1995, p.10.

12. "Ezra Taft Benson," *Ensign*, July 1994, p. 9.

13. Kimball, Spencer W. *The Teachings of Spencer W. Kimball*. Edited by Edward L. Kimball. Salt Lake City, Utah: Bookcraft, 1982. p. 198.

14. *Church Almanac 1997-98*, p. 87-88.

15. Lee, Harold B. *The Teachings of Harold B. Lee*. Edited by Clyde J. Williams. Salt Lake City, Utah: Bookcraft, 1996, p. 422.

16. Address by President Ezra Taft Benson. *Ensign*, Dec. 1988, p 2.

17. Kimball, Edward L., and Andrew E. Kimball, Jr. *Spencer W. Kimball*. Salt Lake City, Utah: Bookcraft, 1977, p. 37.

18. "Loved By All Who Knew Him," *Ensign*, April 1995, p. 19.

19. Brown, Hugh B. *The Abundant Life*. Salt Lake City, Utah: Bookcraft, 1965, p. 337-338.

20. Dew, Sheri L. *Ezra Taft Benson: A Biography*, Deseret Book, 1987, p. 297-298.

21. Kimball, Edward L., and Andrew E. Kimball, Jr. *Spencer W. Kimball*. Salt Lake City, Utah: Bookcraft, 1977, p. 39.

22. Nottingham England Fireside, Aug. 30, 1985. *Teachings of Gordon B. Hinckley*, Deseret Book, p. 559.

23. Address by Brigham Young, *Journal of Discourses*, 12:158.

24. Address by Gordon B. Hinckley, *Ensign*, Nov. 2000, p. 52.

25. Smith, Joseph F. *Gospel Doctrine*. Salt Lake City: Deseret Book, 1939, p.518.

About the authors

Photo courtesy of Ron Douglas

Tammy and Chad Daybell live in Springville, Utah, with their five children.

Tammy Douglas Daybell was born in California and moved to Springville as a teenager. She served as Springville High's yearbook editor and played the drums in the marching band. She attended BYU as an advertising major. Her kids keep her pretty busy, but in her spare time she enjoys reading, gardening, and designing websites.

Chad Daybell was born in Provo, Utah, and was raised in Springville. He served in the New Jersey Morristown Mission among the Spanish-speaking people.

In 1992 he graduated from BYU with a bachelor's degree in journalism, where he served as the City Editor of *The Daily Universe*. Later, he worked as a newspaper editor at *The Standard-Examiner* in Ogden, Utah.

Tammy and Chad longed to have their children grow up closer to their grandparents and extended family, so in 1995 Chad took the unusual step of leaving a newspaper career to become Springville's cemetery sexton. (Chad had worked in the cemetery part-time during college.)

The change of pace actually sparked his imagination, and the plot for the *Emma Trilogy* took shape in his mind. He would work on the novels at night, while pondering the storylines during the day at the cemetery.

By the year 2000, Chad felt a career change was coming his way, and he accepted an offer to manage the Utah division of Access Computer Products. This was a great experience for him, but he soon felt compelled to re-enter the publishing world. In June 2001 he accepted a position as Cedar Fort's managing editor, where he is currently employed.

About the illustrator

Rhett E. Murray received a bachelor's degree from Southern Utah University in Fine Art, and a master's degree from Southern Utah University in Art Education. He also completed a bachelor's degree in fine arts from the Northwest College of Art in Seattle, Washington.

He grew up in Springville, Utah, and served for two years in the Chile Osorno Mission. He lives in Las Vegas, Nevada, with his wife Holly, and their three children. He has taught middle school and high school for the past ten years in Alaska, Washington and Nevada. He is a member of the Nevada Art Guild, and is also a professional portrait artist and illustrator.

Other books by Chad Daybell

The Youth of Zion

This non-fiction book is filled with inspiring stories and quotes from the modern prophets, and gives guidance on more than thirty timely topics facing today's families.

The Emma Trilogy

This award-winning LDS series includes the novels **An Errand for Emma**, **Doug's Dilemma**, and **Escape to Zion.** The novels are exciting time-travel adventures that teach the three missions of the church.

One Foot in the Grave

A humorous collection of strange-but-true stories that occurred while Chad was employed as a cemetery sexton.

Chasing Paradise

Chad's latest novel is a captivating journey that takes place on both sides of the veil. If you liked the Emma Trilogy, you'll love this new book. Available in early 2003.

Visit **www.cdaybell.com** to learn more
about the author and these titles.